Pebble Plus

Exploring the Galaxy

Venus

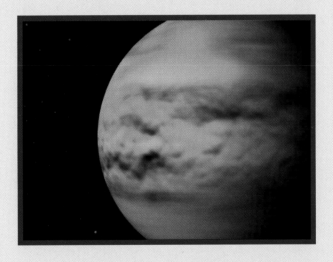

by Thomas K. Adamson

Consulting Editor: Gail Saunders-Smith, Ph.D.

Consultant: James Gerard
Aerospace Education Specialist, NASA
Kennedy Space Center, Florida

Capstone
press

Mankato, Minnesota

Pebble Plus is published by Capstone Press
151 Good Counsel Drive, P.O. Box 669, Mankato, Minnesota 56002
http://www.capstone-press.com

1 2 3 4 5 6 08 07 06 05 04 03

Library of Congress Cataloging-in-Publication Data
Adamson, Thomas K., 1970–
   Venus / by Thomas K. Adamson.
   p. cm.—(Pebble Plus : exploring the galaxy)
   Summary: Simple text and photographs describe the planet Venus.
   Includes bibliographical references and index.
   ISBN 0-7368-2119-8 (hardcover)
   1. Venus (Planet)—Juvenile literature. [1. Venus (Planet)] I. Title. II. Series.
QB621 .A33 2004
523.42—dc21
                                              2002155946

Editorial Credits
Mari C. Schuh, editor; Kia Adams, designer; Alta Schaffer, photo researcher; Eric Kudalis, product planning editor

Photo Credits
Digital Vision, cover, 5 (Venus), 7, 9 (Venus), 15
NASA, 4 (Pluto), 17; JPL, 5 (Jupiter); JPL/Caltech, 5 (Uranus)
PhotoDisc Inc., 4 (Neptune), 5 (Mars, Mercury, Earth, Sun, Saturn), 9 (Earth), 13; Stock Trek, 11; PhotoDisc Imaging, 1, 19
Photo Researchers, Inc./Jerry Schad, 21

Note to Parents and Teachers

The Exploring the Galaxy series supports national science standards related to earth science. This book
describes and illustrates the planet Venus. The photographs support early readers in understanding the
text. The repetition of words and phrases helps early readers learn new words. This book also introduces
early readers to subject-specific vocabulary words, which are defined in the Glossary section. Early readers
may need assistance to read some words and to use the Table of Contents, Glossary, Read More, Internet Sites,
and Index/Word List sections of the book.

Word Count: 118
Early-Intervention Level: 14

Table of Contents

Venus

Venus is the second planet from the Sun. Venus and the other planets move around the Sun.

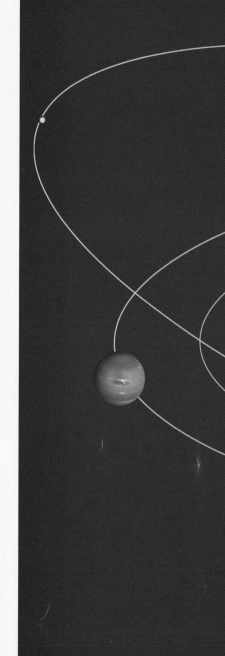

The Solar System

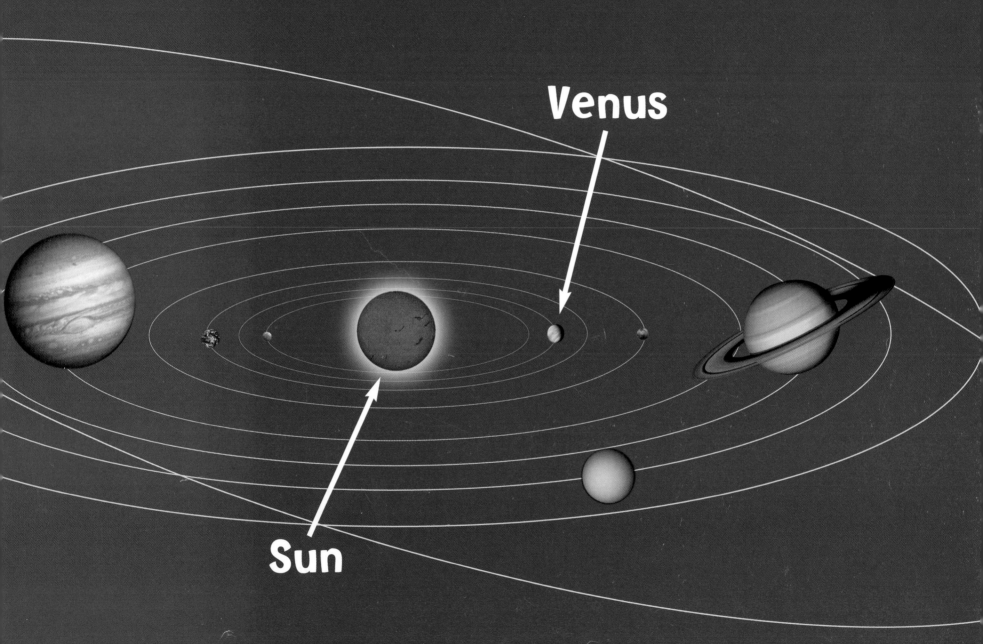

Venus

Sun

Venus is the third brightest
object in the sky. Only
the Sun and Earth's moon
are brighter than Venus.

7

Size of Venus

Venus is almost the
same size as Earth.

Earth

Venus

Air and Land

Venus is the hottest planet.

The surface of Venus

is hotter than an oven.

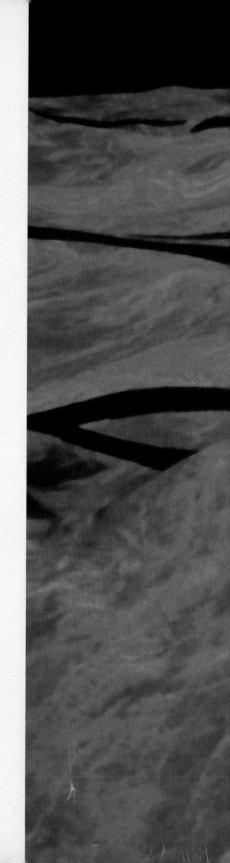

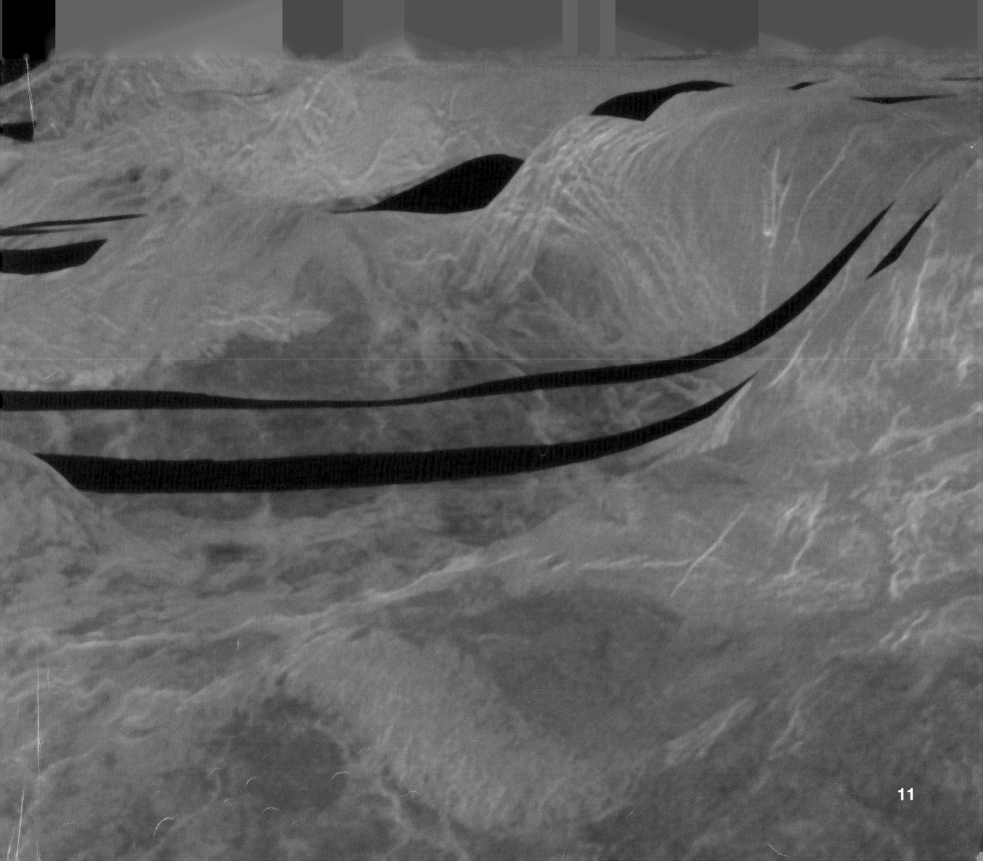

11

Venus has hundreds
of volcanoes. Thousands of
craters cover Venus.

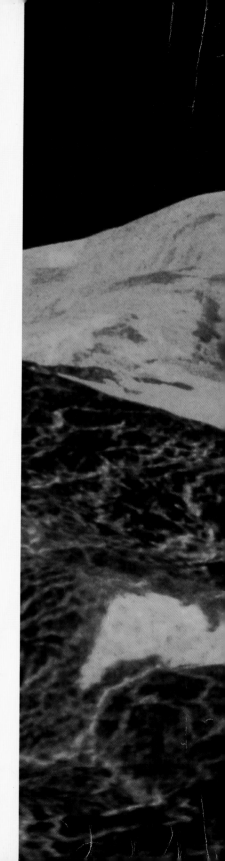

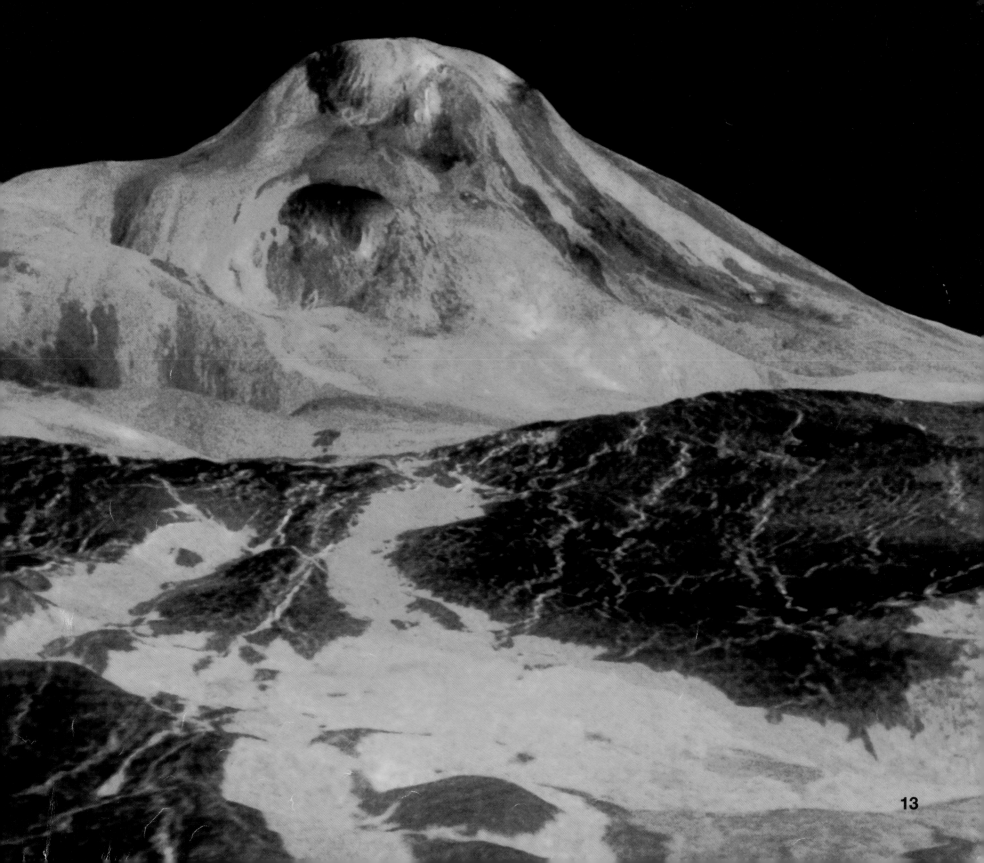

13

Thick clouds made
of acid cover Venus.

The clouds on Venus trap
the Sun's heat. The clouds
make the air heavy.

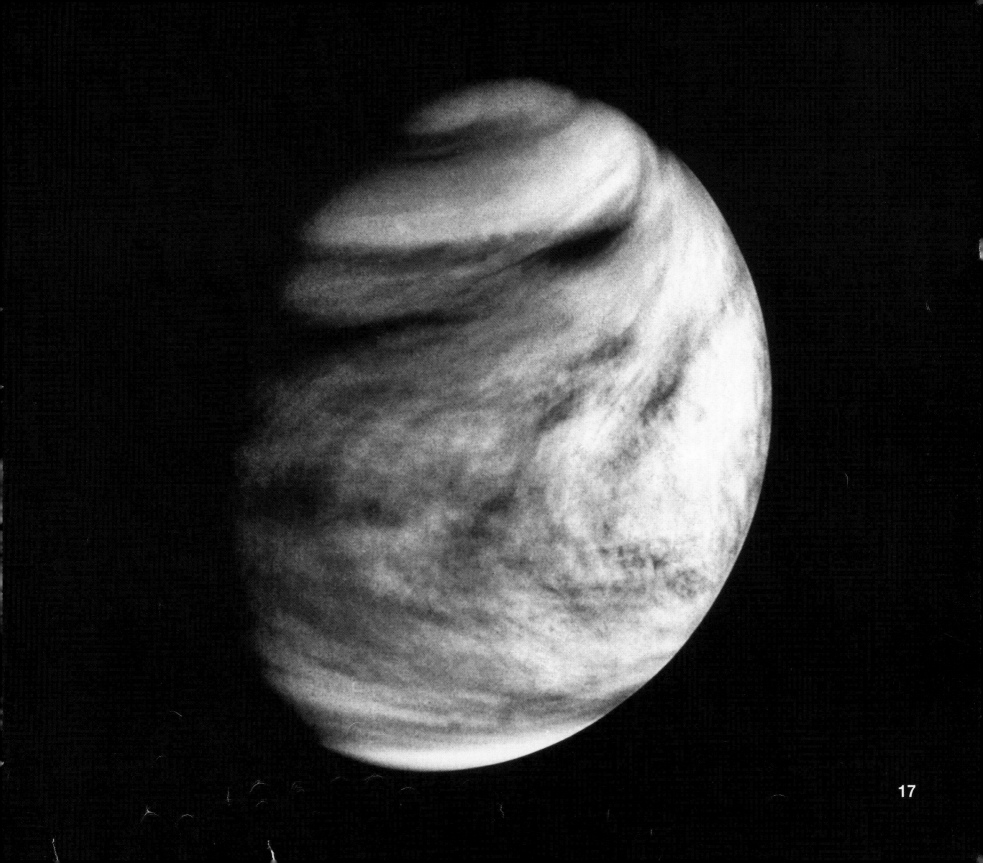

People and Venus

People cannot live on
Venus. The heat would
cook them. The heavy air
would crush them.

People can sometimes see
Venus from Earth. Venus
looks like a bright star.

Venus ←

Glossary

acid—a substance that can harm people

crater—a large hole in the ground; many craters on planets are caused by falling pieces of rock.

oven—an enclosed space, like a stove, where people bake or roast food

planet—a large object that moves around the Sun; Venus is closer to the Sun than Earth is.

Sun—the star that the planets move around; the Sun provides light and heat for the planets.

volcano—a mountain with vents; melted rock oozes out of the vents; volcanoes on Venus are no longer active.

Read More

Cole, Michael D. *Venus: The Second Planet.* Countdown to Space. Berkeley Heights, N.J.: Enslow, 2002.

Goss, Tim. *Venus.* The Universe. Chicago: Heinemann Library, 2002.

Kipp, Steven L. *Venus.* The Galaxy. Mankato, Minn.: Bridgestone Books, 2000.

Internet Sites

Do you want to find out more about Venus and the solar system? Let FactHound, our fact-finding hound dog, do the research for you.

Here's how:

1) Visit *http://www.facthound.com*

2) Type in the **Book ID** number: **0736821198**

3) Click on **FETCH IT**.

FactHound will fetch Internet sites picked by our editors just for you!

Index/Word List